# HE LEADETH ME

THE SHEPHERD'S ROD

# HE LEADETH ME

## Shepherd Life in Palestine— Psalm 23

*By*

### C. W. SLEMMING

**CHRISTIAN LITERATURE CRUSADE**
**Fort Washington, Pennsylvania 19034**

CHRISTIAN LITERATURE CRUSADE

UNITED STATES
P. O. Box 1449, Ft. Washington, PA 19034

First edition 1942
First North American edition 1965
Revised edition 1973


*ISBN 0-87508-505-9*

PRINTED IN THE UNITED STATES OF AMERICA

## PREFACE

TOO few people are acquainted with the habits and customs of Palestine, and so fail to obtain from the Scriptures the first lessons that they are meant to convey. It became my privilege, therefore, to write a little booklet on the Twenty-third Psalm entitled *Echoes from the Hills of Bethlehem*, which revealed much of the habit, custom, and equipment of the Eastern shepherd. This has gone into a number of issues and many testimonies of blessing have come from those who have read it.

With this encouragement the booklet has been enlarged so that the many references to the Shepherd throughout the Bible might be embraced. Many illustrations have now been included which make the book an attractive gift for Birthday, Anniversary, Christmas, for old or young, who will find comfort in the knowledge that the Good Shepherd is ever leading.

C. W. SLEMMING.

"Jesus said,
'I am the Good Shepherd'"

John 10. 11

# FOREWORD

I SUPPOSE that most Christians, at some time or other, have wished they could visit Palestine and walk in those Holy Fields, and study the Bible on the spot, in its Eastern light and setting. For there are many Biblical statements and stories which would be illuminated by such a visit. Alas, it is given only to very few to enjoy this sacred privilege. But here is the next best thing, for the Rev. Chas. W. Slemming, who has given his life to the study of the Bible, particularly in its eastern setting, has produced a most interesting informative volume. In these pages, both obscure and familiar passages are illuminated by Eastern light.

During the last twenty years, hundreds of thousands of people throughout the British Isles have listened spell-bound to his now famous lecture " An Eastern Shepherd ". It makes *The Book* live before our eyes, and we become eye- as well as ear-witnesses. Here is a book to place in the hand of a young convert ; but it will also enable the mature Christian to rejoice in the Holy Word. It contains a message for the unconverted also, and Christians do well to speed its circulation in evangelism. It has been a pleasure to work in the closest co-operation with my friend Mr. Slemming in all parts of the Land and I commend this volume on its mission. I believe it will be the means of bringing blessing and inspiration to a very large number of people throughout the English-speaking world.

F. T. ELLIS.

## LIST OF ILLUSTRATIONS

and numerous illustrations in the Text.

# CONTENTS

E.A.S

## ITS PLACE IN THE SCRIPTURES

WHAT an entrancing subject is shepherd life in Palestine! Its scenes absorb us with interest at every turn of the way. The Bible narrative is full of illustration concerning shepherds and sheep so that, if we know something of their life and experiences, we shall be able the better to understand many portions of these Scriptures which otherwise appear only to be in the abstract. One of the reasons why there are so many references and allusions in the Bible is the fact that Palestine, the land of the Bible, is primarily an agricultural country, so that sheep are abundant and shepherds many, therefore everyone there would understand the language used. The earliest reference goes back to the beginning of time: " And Abel was a keeper of sheep " (Genesis 4. 2), while the last reference is found in 1 Peter 5. 4: "And when the chief Shepherd shall appear, ye shall receive a crown of glory that fadeth not away." And what of the many choice Scriptures between these two, in Old and New Testaments alike? Let us call to our memory a few of them for they will warm our hearts to the subject. There is, of course, the outstanding gem of the Psalms (23) "The Lord is my Shepherd, I shall not want", the Psalm known by young and old, learnt by the child at its Mother's knees, chanted by the saints as a song of praise, read by the believer in the hour of need or danger, and uttered with the dying breath of many who have gone before. This Psalm has been, and is, precious because firstly, it is Divine and, secondly, it is practical.

Other gems of the Old Testament writings are: "He shall feed His flock like a Shepherd: He shall gather the lambs with His arm, and carry them in His bosom, and shall gently lead those that are with young" (Isaiah 40. 11). Again: "All we like sheep have gone astray" (Isaiah 53. 6), and: "As a sheep before her shearers is dumb, so opened He not His mouth" (Isaiah 53. 7).

In the New Testament we have the shepherds abiding in the fields who received the angelic messengers with the good news that unto them (and us) was born in the City of David a Saviour who was Christ the Lord; the parable of the lost sheep in Luke 15, and the beautiful chapter of John (10) where Jesus says: "I am the Good Shepherd." One of the New Testament benedictions is: "Now the God of peace, that brought again from the dead our Lord Jesus, that Great Shepherd of the sheep, through the blood of the everlasting covenant, make you perfect in every good work to do His will, working in you that which is wellpleasing in His sight, through Jesus Christ; to whom be glory for ever and ever, Amen" (Hebrews 13. 20–21).

"—AND CARRY THEM IN HIS BOSOM"

Coming back to the Psalms, it has been pointed out that Psalms 22, 23 and 24, all belong to the Shepherd:—

Psalm 22 the Good Shepherd dying for His sheep,
Psalm 23 the Great Shepherd living for His sheep,
Psalm 24 the Chief Shepherd coming for His sheep.

While there are numerous other Scriptures all alive with suggestiveness, and a glance at a Concordance would call them to your memory, yet the inspired writers used the same shepherds as a warning note of failure and judgment, particularly in Ezekiel 34 and Zechariah 11: "Son of man, prophesy against the shepherds of Israel, prophesy, and say unto them, Thus saith the Lord God unto the shepherds; Woe be to the shepherds of Israel that do feed themselves! Should not the shepherds feed the flocks?" etc., etc. May we heed the warnings as well as receive the blessings.

Abraham, Lot, Jacob, Joseph's brethren, Moses, David are among the well-known men who kept sheep.

Let us now journey with a shepherd of Bethlehem and his flock and see what we can glean from their experiences that will help us to understand the Bible as well as comprehend a little more of the Great Shepherd of the sheep. We will divide our thoughts into three main divisions to help us harness the many experiences and the numerous references. They will be Sunrise, Noonday, Eventide.

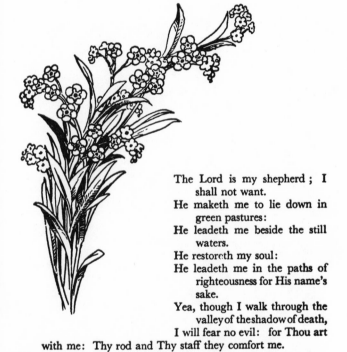

The Lord is my shepherd ; I shall not want.

He maketh me to lie down in green pastures:

He leadeth me beside the still waters.

He restoreth my soul:

He leadeth me in the paths of righteousness for His name's sake.

Yea, though I walk through the valley of the shadow of death,

I will fear no evil: for Thou art with me: Thy rod and Thy staff they comfort me.

Thou preparest a table before me in the presence of mine enemies:

Thou anointest my head with oil ; my cup runneth over.

Surely goodness and mercy shall follow me all the days of my life:

And I will dwell in the house of the Lord for ever.

(PSALM 23).

"And when the Chief Shepherd shall appear, ye shall receive a crown of glory that fadeth not away."

1 Peter 5. 4

## SUNRISE

With the rising of the sun the shepherds are astir and ready to move forward with their flocks before the sun gets too high in the sky and the heat too intense. Let us look first at

THE SHEPHERD. " The Lord is My Shepherd."

He is so different from the shepherd of the Western world. It is usually the youngest son who is appointed to this task because it is considered low and menial. You will remember that David was the youngest son of Jesse and he was away in the fields tending the sheep when Samuel the prophet called at the home to anoint a King for Israel. Not being successful in his search as one by one the brethren came and went, he enquired as to whether there was not yet another son. One can almost hear the sneer and see the disdain of those older brothers as Jesse said: " There remaineth yet the youngest and, behold, he keepeth the sheep." " Send and fetch him," said the prophet, and so David was brought from the sheepcotes and anointed King of Israel (1 Samuel 16).

If a man had only one son, then the daughters would be made shepherdesses. So it was that Rachel, the youngest daughter of Laban, looked after her father's sheep (Genesis 29. 9). Jethro's daughters also looked after the sheep (Exodus 2. 16). It is interesting to note in the next chapter (Exodus 3) that Moses takes the place of these daughters. He had to learn to lead sheep before he could lead a nation.

There is an exception that proves the rule, and at the same time explains the reason for a domestic quarrel. It is the story of Joseph. He was in the fields tending the flocks with his brethren when, at the age of seventeen, Jacob chose to recall Joseph because of his peculiar love for him and to give to him that coat which designated him as heir, so that he remained at home when, according to custom, he should have tended the flock while his older brethren should have been in the army or at home. This naturally created the jealousy which in turn gendered hatred that brought the thought of murder.

These references to the humble lot of a shepherd have been pointed out because they enhance the already beautiful testimony of the Lord: " I am the Good Shepherd."

Not only is the position a *lowly* one but it is also a *lonely* one. A shepherd leaving home will be away for weeks at a stretch knowing no other companionship but that of his sheep and the occasional meeting with other shepherds. They have to keep moving on because the pastures are at times scarce. Thus it was that when Joseph went to Shechem he found the brethren had moved on to Dothan. Our Good Shepherd knew something of loneliness: " They all forsook Him and fled." He trod the winepress alone.

ROBBERS

(*See page* 58)

With these thoughts in our mind we can understand how it was that David, sitting with his flock and seeing their contentment, could look heavenwards and say: " The Lord is My Shepherd." Who is this Shepherd ? The Lord—Jehovah. David refers to the first Person of the Trinity, the God of the Old Testament Saints. In John 10, the Lord Jesus, the Second Person of the Holy Trinity, says: " I am the Good Shepherd," while to-day, in this dispensation of the Holy Spirit, we find the Spirit doing exactly the same thing—winning, wooing, leading, so that within this statement can be seen the whole Triune God. What wonderful condescension! What love! Why did He become a Shepherd ? There are three reasons among the many that we would just mention. (1) Because all we like sheep had gone astray and were, therefore, in need of a Shepherd to lead us. (2) Because God would not entrust the care of His Sheep to an hireling, knowing that sometimes " the hireling fleeth because he is an hireling and careth not for the sheep ". (3) Because He was a Son and the only Son, God could trust Him. What has the Shepherd done for the sheep ? (1) He has given His life for the Sheep. (2) He has become the door into the sheepfold (John 10. 2). (3) He has given His Sheep eternal life. (4) He will keep them for ever. " No man shall pluck them out of My Hand." Who are His Sheep ? John gives to us three wonderful characteristics that mark out these Sheep. (1) They hear His voice (John 10. 27). (2) They know Him (John 10. 14). (3) They follow Him (John 10. 27). Those that hear Him, know Him, and follow Him, are those who can say: " The Lord is my Shepherd."

THE DRESS.

Much is similar to that worn by the Fellaheen (the country folk) with one exception—instead of the outer *abba* the shepherd sometimes wears a fleece coat. The story is told of a shepherd once being asked why he wore a sheep-skin, to which he replied; " My sheep like to see me looking like one of themselves." This answer may have been very sentimental but we know that it is true that the Lord became like one of ourselves, and took upon Himself the form of man and, in addition, He took upon Himself our nature and was tempted in all points as we are, and so He is able to succour those who are tempted. The actual reason for the shepherd wearing a fleece is twofold. It is to keep him warm and to keep him cool. This indeed sounds a paradox, but it is true. Palestine weather is very severe in its change. It is possible to have a temperature of over 100° in the shade by day and frost the same night. A suggestion of this is found in the words of Jacob to Laban: " Thus it was, in the day the drought consumed me and the frost by night " (Genesis 31. 40). The natural oil in the skin protects him from the heat of the sun while, reversing his coat at night, the wool is his warmth. Before leaving the fold let us take note of the variety of

# THE EQUIPMENT.

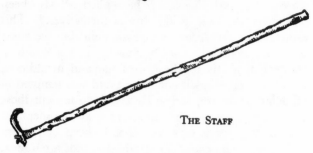

THE STAFF

**The Rod and Staff.** We will only but make mention of them here as we shall see them in use as presently we journey with the shepherd. The Rod is used as a weapon of protection for the sheep against their enemies. The Staff is for rescuing the entrapped lamb and for guiding purposes—hence their comfort.

SLING

**The Sling,** often made by the shepherd himself, is the weapon of the offensive. It is used to keep the enemy at bay. It also acts as a sheep-dog.

**The scrip.** This is a bag made from the skin of a kid of the goats. In it the shepherd carries all his small belongings and his food. He lives principally on berries, locusts, and wild honey—things he would find on his journeys.

**A Bottle of Hog's Oil** as a protection against vipers.

**A Reed Flute** with which he entertains himself and passes away his hours. On one of these no doubt David composed some of his Psalms.

PIPE

**A Lamp.** This is a long lamp made of parchment and folded into its top and bottom like a chinese lantern. Lighting the little oil lamp inside the shepherd holds it so as to give light to his feet as in the dark he journeys one step at a time.

This completes his equipment.

LAMP

## SETTING OUT FOR THE DAY.

Inside the fold there are possibly several flocks of sheep, all of them mixed together as one flock.

"*He leadeth me.*" When ready to journey one of the shepherds steps outside the fold and calls his sheep. Immediately there is a twisting and turning, and from the many out file that shepherd's sheep and gather around his feet, none but his own come out and not one of his own remains inside. After this another shepherd comes out and stands aside, using the same call exactly as the other man. His sheep file out and assemble themselves together. How is it done? The Scriptures tell us: "For they know His voice." The story is told of the Rev. Samuel Schor, who was a native of Jerusalem and who acquainted himself quite a bit with shepherds, asking a shepherd on one occasion if he might call the sheep, assuring the man that he was a good imitator of voices. He called, but the sheep, having looked up, continued with their grazing. "I think they must have recognized me," said Mr. Schor. "Allow me to put on your clothes." The shepherd agreed, and Mr. Schor called again but with no better result. Here now is the whole text: "And when He putteth forth His own sheep, He goeth before them, and the sheep follow Him: for they know His voice. And a stranger will they not follow, but will flee from him: *for they know not the voice of strangers*" (John 10. 4–5).

"He leadeth Me"

This text of Scripture makes known another great truth of Eastern shepherd life, that is: "He goeth before them." In this country sheep are always driven, in Palestine they are always led. The Shepherd saunters along according to the condition of his sheep, and they follow. He "gently leads those that are with young" doing his journey in easy stages. An English guide who was conducting a party of tourists through the Holy Land had made known to them the fact that shepherds always led their sheep, when one day one of the party called the guide's attention to a flock of sheep being driven, remarking: "I thought you said it was never done." "That is so," said the guide, "I think we ought to enquire." Going across to the man, he said: "Excuse me, Mr. Shepherd, why are you driving your sheep? I thought it was never done?" The man looked at him, then said: "Shepherd? I'm not a shepherd—I'm a butcher!" So the exception proved the rule! What a wonderful truth! Christ is NOT a butcher, He is a Shepherd. That means the Lord will never drive you against your will, He never forces you to do the thing you do not wish to do. He has given us a will, and He will respect that will. While He does not drive, He does all He can to encourage and to persuade. One of the reasons why we have wars, etc., is that man wills to go his own way and God allows him. If God took from us will-power, we would become automatons—machinery forced by a great power. Therefore never blame God for wars and their results, blame man. God is able as far as His power is concerned, but God will not as far as man's liberty is concerned. These things apply to salvation, to surrender, and to service.

1. **The Leader.** " HE leadeth me." In the morning he leads them out of the fold into the meadows that are fresh with the dew. At noonday, when the sun is high, he leads them into the shelter of a rock or into some other place of coolness, thus bringing them protection; in the evening he leads them on again, bringing them into the fold and then becoming the door of the fold keeping the wolf and bear at bay. Even so we are able to say: " HE leadeth me." In the morning of life, with all the vigour of youth, He leads us into the freshness of life with all its charms and attractions. When we mature to manhood and take up the responsibilities of life, thus bearing the heat and burden of the day, then we still know Him as the Shepherd. He will share our burdens and lead us into His own Divine protection. In the closing scenes of life He will not forsake us but will lead us onward and upward into the rest that remaineth to the people of God. We will find that He leads us *by His Word*: " Thy Word is a lamp unto my feet," *by our circumstances*: " All things work together for good to them that love God," *by His Spirit*: " When He, the Spirit of Truth, is come, He will guide you into all truth."

2. **The Led.** " He leadeth ME." The personal pronouns are very beautiful—HE and ME, this was the personal testimony of David, and we can use it as ours. He leads me because I am willing to follow, and because I keep my eyes on Him.

3. **The Path.** " Paths of Righteousness." This comes as a natural result of restoration. If we find ourselves in dangerous or barren places with our souls exposed to dangers, and our spirit languishing for want of spirituality, it is certainly because we have wandered as erring sheep. The Lord would never lead us into

such places. Having restored our souls, He leads us along paths of rightness. Look back on your path of life, cannot you count your Ebenezers, the times the Lord has guided you into paths of blessing? Notice the plurality of the word. Not one path but many. Some of those many paths into which the Lord leads are:—

(a) *The Path of Peace.* His paths are peace and plenty. It is a peace such as the world knows not.

(b) *The Path of Prayer.* How many are the blessings which come to us through this particular avenue.

(c) *The Path of Power.* This path is marked out by the Lord. All power is given unto ME—go ye and preach.

(d) *The Path of Progression.* It is not keeping us in a certain place but leading us along paths of righteousness.

E.A.S

**4. The Reason.** "For his Name's sake." Have
you ever noticed that God works always on our behalf
for "Jesus' sake". What is His Name? Here it is
Shepherd—if He fails to care and lead, He fails to be a
Shepherd. Therefore, He must care for us because
His Name demands it. Christ has many other Names
beside that of Shepherd, seven of which can be found
here in this Psalm. They are;—

Jehovah Rohi—The Lord is My Shepherd—" The Lord
is My Shepherd."

Jehovah Jireh—The Lord will Provide—" I shall not
want."

Jehovah Shalom—The Lord send Peace—" He leadeth
me beside still waters."

Jehovah Rophi—The Lord that Healeth—" He restoreth my soul."

Jehovah Tsidkenu—The Lord our Righteousness—
" Paths of righteousness."

Jehovah Shammah—The Lord is There—" Thou art
with me."

Jehovah Nissi—The Lord my Banner—" In the presence of mine enemies."


**Green Pastures.** Having left the fold and travelled
on with the shepherd a little way, maybe he decides to
bring his sheep to a halt. The flock is still fairly fresh ;
perhaps they are restive and do not want to rest,
so he *makes* them " to lie down in green pastures ".
Why a rest so soon? Why a rest when apparently the
sheep do not want one? The reason is that the
shepherd can see much farther ahead than the sheep,
and he has noticed a very long steep climb along a
narrow and dangerous path to a mountain height. It is
the only path to be taken and, should he go straight
away to it, some of the flock might tire and there would

be a risk of them falling from the narrow way. The rest, therefore, will reinvigorate, and so enable the sheep to go right through the strenuous climb. Let us sit down with the shepherd and ponder this thought, it will be worth while. What a blessing for those sheep that they have such a kind and interested shepherd, whose one thought is always their welfare. Are we not the sheep of His pasture? Is He not the Good Shepherd? Will He do less for us than the ordinary shepherd does for his sheep? Nay! Your comfort and mine is that our Shepherd can see very much farther than we can, He sees the end from the beginning. His great Heart of Love is ever planning for us with an eternal wisdom. Are there not times in our experiences when the Lord has sought to bring us to a place of rest and repose saying; " In quietness and in confidence shall be your strength" (Isaiah 30. 15), and we have become restless. We are living in an age of rush and turmoil. Life is very hectic and its demands are very severe, we are much too busy to rest. There is service to be rendered, and a fight to be fought. We feel sometimes that we are indispensable and ofttimes, becoming exhausted, we " fall beside the way and faint ". Even as the physical body must have periods of rest if it is to continue in a really energetic condition, so must the soul find its repose in the Lord. This need not necessarily be inactivity, although sometimes it does really mean that. So it is that he *makes* us to lie down, not in barren places but in green pastures. Note the word " maketh ", not force but gentle persuasion. Our slogan becomes " Activity ", and so for our good He touches " the hollow of our thigh " and causes us to rest.

36

"HE MAKETH ME TO LIE DOWN"

Do you say that rest is wasted time? No! No!!
The hymn-writer expressed the truth when he said:

Come ye and rest, the journey is too great,
And ye will faint beside the way, and sink;
The Bread of Life is here for you to eat,
And here for you the Wine of Love to drink.
Then, fresh from converse with your Lord, return
And work till daylight softens into even;
The brief hours are not lost in which ye learn
More of your Master and His rest in heaven.

Be willing, therefore, to submit without pressure. " Be
still and know that I am God." He turns us from the
rush of the commonplace to the hush of communion,
because he always plans for us to-day with His eye on
to-morrow.

Away from the great quest of life into exile and John,
in Patmos, wrote the Revelation of Jesus Christ: away
from the activities of life, laid aside in the sick chamber,
Frances Ridley Havergal has given inspiration to
thousands through her sanctified pen. While some
return not from their confinement, many find seclusion
only to be temporary.

Possibly this is one of the hardest lessons of life. It is
as difficult to hold some people back as it is to persuade
others to go forward. The one can be as big a danger
as the other. This snare is met more by the younger
folk. We sometimes feel so confident that we are
inclined to push aside the sound advice of the more
sober and matured Christian, only to learn later that
they were right and we were wrong.

Let us take to heart this word of admonition given
to us by the same shepherd who wrote the 23rd Psalm:
" Wait on the Lord; be of good courage and He shall
strengthen thine heart; wait, I say, on the Lord "
(Psalm 27. 14). The result of this waiting, this repose,
is given us by Isaiah, who said: " They that wait upon
the Lord shall renew their strength; they shall mount

up with wings as eagles; they shall run, and not be weary; and they shall walk, and not faint."

While we are resting here with the shepherd, may we meditate on another thought expressed by David in the 23rd Psalm. He said;—*He restoreth my soul*. The word " restoreth " is MESHIBAH in the Hebrew and is sometimes translated " Converting ", as in Psalm 19. 7: " The law of the Lord is perfect converting (restoring) the soul." There are several phases of restoration for which this word stands. In Psalm 80. 19 it is restoration from disorder and decay. In Ruth 4. 15 it is restoration from sorrow and affliction, while in 1 Kings 17. 21–22 it is restoration from death as Elijah restored to life the child which was dead. So we learn that there is a restoration which revives drooping hearts and fainting bodies, and there is a restoration from waywardness for those who find themselves at a distance. David was certainly speaking from experience for we know that there was a time when he had lost the joy of his salvation, and he prayed that the Lord would restore it unto him (Psalm 51. 12).

Let us ask ourselves three questions in this connection:—

## 1. **When is restoration needed**

(a) *When we are weak and fainting.* David said: "HE restoreth my soul." It was not a tonic but a person. So many people think that a little of the lighter side of life will put the soul of a Church right. They would suggest that if spiritual and physical vitalities are low, social hours, clubs, etc., will restore, but they usually prove to be a drug that nullifies conscience completely. The Lord said that HE would restore the years that the cankerworm and the caterpillar had eaten.

(b) *When there is a backsliding state.* When the soul loses its first love, we can be sure that the feet will follow the desire, so that immediately there is a waywardness which makes us ask our second question:—

## 2. **What are the symptoms of backsliding**

(a) *Following afar off.* The sheep that follow at a distance are at a greater peril than those which walk near at hand. The fear, of which Scripture says that it is a snare to the soul, can sometimes be the cause of distance. Our weakness in testimony ofttimes robs us of our joy and so we become—

(b) *Discontented and Restless.* This is an unhealthy condition. Discontentment brings irritability, the result of which is a murmuring against the Church, the Minister, the ministry, the Saints. In their restlessness, discontented people wander about. But the old saying remains true: "A rolling stone gathers no moss," and an irregularity in attendance leads to a non-attendance. With these things comes a—

(c) *Neglect of the Word of God.* The thoughts of men take the place of the thoughts of God, and His thoughts

40

are not our thoughts. When David did this he complained at the prosperity of the wicked. What a comfort these words " HE restoreth my soul " are as they come from the pen of the man who thus complained. The final question is:—

3. **How is restoration effected**   There are two methods:—

(*a*) *By the shepherd's look.*   This was seen in Peter's life. The Lord looked upon Peter, He did not speak. It was possibly a look of disappointment, which can be more hurtful to the soul than a look of anger or of reprimand.

(*b*) *By the shepherd's crook.*   We will not tarry on this aspect at the moment as we shall consider it presently, so let us arise now and journey on with the shepherd.

O Zion, that bringest good tidings, get thee up into the high mountain; O Jerusalem, that bringest good tidings, lift up thy voice with strength ; lift *it* up, be not afraid ; say unto the cities of Judah, Behold your God !

Behold, the Lord God will come with strong *hand*, and His arm shall rule for Him : behold, His reward *is* with Him, and His work before Him.

He shall feed His flock like a shepherd : He shall gather the lambs with His arm, and carry *them* in His bosom, *and* shall gently lead those that are with young.

(ISAIAH 40. 9–11).

CAMELS ARE ANOINTED WITH OIL  (*See page* 54)

## NOONDAY

Many are the experiences witnessed and many are the enemies encountered. These we shall seek to consider in turn.

STILL WATERS. " Beside the Still Waters."

Having reached the mountain-top the sheep are hot and thirsty. It may be that there is water in abundance gushing from a rock, or bounding over rocks and making its way swiftly down the side of the mountain: but this would not meet the need of the sheep, they could perish from thirst while water is abundant because they cannot drink from fast running water. It becomes necessary for the shepherd to find a hollowed rock or something that will hold water and then he will bale it from the running stream into the receptacle or, if it be gushing from a rock, with his staff he will scratch a channel in the earth from the water for a little distance and, hollowing the earth, the water will trickle along the channel,

43

fill up the hollow, and so he has made a pool of "still waters". From this, and others that he will make, the sheep drink.

Christ's Love is like torrential waters. His Grace is like a swelling tide. Who can approach the height and depth, length and breadth of the Love of God? It passeth understanding; it is beyond our comprehension, but from it comes that life-giving stream from which you and I find refreshment. God's Word, too, is like a great torrent. The depths of its mysteries will never be fathomed, the height of its glory never attained, the vastness of its wonders never discovered. It is a mine never to be exhausted, a spring never to run dry. It is the unsearchable riches of His grace but, whilst it remains beyond all human comprehension, we thank God for the still waters of that Word to which we have been led and of which we have partaken, and we shall anticipate the day when we shall be able to eat of the hidden manna and drink of the fountain head.

FEEDING. "Thou Preparest a Table before Me."

Much is said in Scripture concerning the feeding of the flock. One of the outstanding chapters is Ezekiel 34 where God reproves the shepherds of Israel for failing to discharge their obligations. They fed themselves but not their sheep. He then goes on to say: " I will feed them in a good pasture, and upon the high mountains of Israel shall their fold be: there shall they lie in a good fold, and in a fat pasture shall they feed upon the mountains of Israel. I will feed my flock, and will cause them to lie down, saith the Lord God " (v. 14–15). Peter exhorts the elders of the Church to " Feed the flock of God which is among you " (1 Peter 5. 2).

Not only does the shepherd lead his sheep into the best of pastures but, as he journeys, he notices high on the banks, perhaps beyond the reach of the sheep, sweet and juicy herbs such as sheep like. These he plucks.

" Beside the Still Waters "

Then, too, high on the trees will be leaves or fruit, again tasty tit-bits for the sheep, and so up goes his staff and, pulling a branch, he breaks off those morsels. A picture indeed for those who are called to be God's under-Shepherds, bringing the food to the level and reach of the flock. In either case the shepherd never throws to the ground the things he gathers. He holds them in his hand behind him and the sheep nibble them from his hand as he ambles on in front of them. One need not ask the question; " Which sheep ? " It is so obvious—those that walk nearest. My dear friend, it does really pay to walk near to the Good Shepherd of the sheep. It is those who walk nearest who receive all the revelations, all the joys, all the deep and real experiences of fellowship with Him.

## " IN THE PRESENCE OF MINE ENEMIES "

Another experience met by the Eastern Shepherd as he seeks to feed his flock is that sometimes he comes to a field which is infested with vipers. They are little brown adders which live under the ground. They have a way of coming up out of their little holes, nipping the noses of the sheep and thereby poisoning them so that the sheep die. The shepherd's method of dealing with this situation is to leave the sheep outside any such infested field while he takes from his girdle a bottle of hog's oil. Then, scanning the field and raking over any long grass with his rod, he pours a circle of the oil around every hole he can find. The sheep are then allowed to enter and graze. As soon as the vipers beneath the ground realize that there are sheep above, up they come out of their holes but only to find they can get no farther. The smooth bodies of the vipers cannot pass over the slippery oil, so they are prisoners inside the circle. " But," you say, " If the vipers cannot get near to the sheep, the sheep can get near to the vipers." No! For when the noses of the sheep get near to that oil they turn immediately in another direction for they do not like the smell. Now it was to this little scene that the Psalmist referred when he said: " Thou preparest a table before me in the presence of mine enemies."

Some people have thought that the 23rd Psalm changed part way through from a Pastoral Scene to a Palace Banquet, but that is not so. It remains the same to the end. You see the shepherd preparing the field and then the sheep grazing while the vipers look on. " The angel of the Lord encampeth round about them that fear Him." As the shepherd surrounds the hole with oil, even so has the Lord surrounded us with the oil of the Holy Ghost. Cannot we all say " Amen " to this ? How many tables has the Lord prepared for us in the midst of our enemies ? It will suffice here to mention three of them.

(1) **Our Daily Bread**. " Every good and every perfect gift cometh from above." Our quota of food has come to us every day, and our needs have been supplied ofttimes in the presence of enemies. Drought, frosts, blight and plague have often threatened our harvest, and men have begun to fear, but the promise

has remained true: " While the earth remaineth, seed-time and harvest, and cold and heat, and summer and winter, and day and night shall not cease " (Genesis 8. 22):—

> He daily spreads a glorious feast,
> And at His tables dine
> The whole creation, man and beast,
> And He's a friend of mine.

(2) **The Holy Scriptures.** What a feast of fat things lies before us when we turn over the pages of the Word of God. In it there is corn, manna, honey, wine and milk, also strong meat. It is the best and is supplied in abundance. It matters not what my need is, or what my circumstance in life may be, here is my source of supply. I can sit and feed upon the Word of God in the presence of such enemies as the Modernist, the Sceptic, the Critic, the Infidel, the Agnostic—yes! even the Devil himself, and none can prevent because both the Book and its reader are encircled with the oil of the Holy Ghost as He, the Spirit of Truth, leads into all truth.

(3) **The Lord's Table.** Here we partake of Him, feasting upon the bread which is His Body and drinking the wine which is His Blood: and this we do while enemies are denying His meritorious Death and the efficacy of His precious Blood.

These, and other tables, are prepared by the Lord Himself—" THOU preparest ".

Yet again, it is a PREPARED TABLE—not a snack-bar, nor a running buffet, but a prepared set-out meal. We can sit quietly and meditate, we can partake and enjoy with the utmost confidence.

> Then, fresh from converse with your Lord, return
> And work till daylight softens into even,
> The brief hours are not lost in which ye learn
> More of your Master and His rest in heaven.

Let us journey on with the shepherd and note other of the enemies he meets and his method of dealing with them.

" Five smooth stones "

**Wild Animals,** as the lion and the bear of which David spoke when talking to Saul about going out to meet Goliath. To keep these animals at a distance and so protect the sheep, the shepherd carries always a sling. This he learns to use with great skill, his accuracy of aim is remarkable. The same applied to soldiers so that we read: " Among all this people there were seven hundred chosen men left-handed; everyone could sling stones at an hair breadth and not miss" (Judges 20. 16).

It was with the sling that the shepherd of Bethlehem became the champion of Israel on the occasion when, in the Name of the Lord, he went out to meet Goliath. People with critical minds have sought to reason out as to which stone it was that killed the giant. Be assured that if a shepherd boy should miss such a large target the first time no giant would stay to give him a second chance! To this sometimes comes the reply that David must have had little faith to take five stones. It was not David's faith that was at fault, but our own reading of Scripture that is defective, for the Bible tells us that the giant had four sons, all of whom fell at the hand of David (2 Sam. 21. 22)! Thus he went forth prepared to meet every obstacle, and so ought we.

While thinking of the sling may we point out that it has yet another use. The shepherd uses it as much for the sheep as for the enemy. Should the flock be scattered, or should one of the sheep be roaming at a distance, then the shepherd puts a stone into his sling and discharges it with such skill that the stone would fall just the other side of the sheep, causing it to startle with alarm and run back to the shepherd for protection. What a wonderful picture! There are times when we get a little cold in spiritual things and are not enjoying

USING SLING

that close fellowship : maybe we have sought our own pastures and have unconsciously wandered. In such circumstances the Lord sometimes drops one of those stones of alarm nearby, perhaps in a permitted sickness, a business problem, a domestic sorrow, a bereavement, a score of different things, but in this way or that He is awaking our consciences and so driving us back to Himself. We ought to thank Him for these awakenings for they prove His Love. " Whom the Father loveth, He chasteneth." Surely this is a comforting thought!

While the sling is used to keep the enemy at a distance, should his keen eye have failed to observe the approach of the enemy, then it would mean close combat. Here the Rod comes into use, or the " Nabbuteh", as he calls it. When one sees the formidable club-like weapon, one is inclined at first to wonder what David meant when he said: " Thy rod and Thy staff they comfort me "—" Comfort " would be the thought farthest from our mind! But upon reflection we remember that David had taken the place of a lamb, saying: " The Lord is my Shepherd," and the rod was never used on any of the sheep but always on the enemy. It was no doubt this rod that had been brought into action against the bear which David had taken by the beard and slain. As the sheep have no fear of the enemy while the shepherd has his rod in his hand, so we need not fear all those who seek to raise up their heads against us, whether they be national enemies or spiritual foes because we read in the " Psalm of the Son ": " Ask of Me, and I shall give thee the heathen for thine inheritance, and the uttermost parts of the earth for thy possession. Thou shalt break them with a rod of iron; thou shalt dash them in pieces like a potter's vessel " (Psalm 2. 8–9).

The use of the rod reminds us of another enemy occasionally met. It is in the form of

**Thorns, Briars, and Thistles.** There are stretches of land in Palestine that are sometimes overgrown with these weeds which ever remind us of sin. To go round would possibly mean a long detour, to go through would mean that the animals would be badly torn and scratched. The way out is the way through, however, so the shepherd still leading the way takes his rod into his hand and swings it from right to left as he moves forward. In so doing he will beat down those thorns and thus make a path right through the infested land. The sheep, which are following behind, walk along this newly made path with those briars on either side of them but they themselves are untouched. Is this not a beautiful picture of Romans 6. 14; " For sin shall not have dominion over you." While the briars of sin and temptation would seek to claw at our souls, we can journey through this present evil world unmolested providing we walk in the footsteps of the Great Shepherd. Then, too, there are

**Snares** into which sheep can easily run. One of these is the attraction to long and juicy grass. As the flock moves forward a lamb may notice away to one side this attractive meal. Making its way to it, it will feed contentedly going a little farther and farther, not realizing that it is getting more and more entangled beneath a great thorn bush. It is the shade of this bush that has kept the grass fresh. When the uncautious lamb has finished eating there and seeks to return, it finds that it cannot back out: it is made a prisoner beneath the bush. Fortunately for the lamb the shepherd carries his staff, or his " Assayeh ", which he will hook around one of the legs of the lamb and thereby gently ease it out. " Thy Staff it comforts me "—yes, indeed!

There are many cults and "isms" abroad to-day that lure men with a certain amount of truth which is served in an attractive form, but behind the truth are the thorns of error which ensnares, "cunningly devised fables" the apostle calls them. How we ever need to be on our guard! How necessary to keep to the narrow path! Friend, if you have been guiled like a foolish lamb, your Shepherd has a staff—it is the Word of His Truth—let Him deliver you.

**Sunstroke** is another of the enemies encountered and so we read: "Thou anointest my head with oil; my cup runneth over." Yet once more we step back into the "Land of the Book" to understand the real use of oil. Both camels and sheep are anointed with oil on their heads to prevent them from sunstroke, as so often there is no protection to be found. Sometimes Arabs have failed to observe this duty, with the result that their camels collapse in the desert and die of sunstroke. Anointing is suggestive, therefore, of protection from opposing elements, hence the Holy Spirit is likened to both oil and anointing. He was bequeathed to us as a Guide and Comforter.

In the Old Testament men were anointed to office with oil, both to Kingship and Priesthood. It was the seal of God's consecration of these men to His service. A priest, without his anointing, missed the chief qualification for his office. We are all of us the sheep of His pasture, and we are also called to be Priests. The oil was not applied to sheep once only, and so it is that we, as the servants of God, need a fresh anointing of God's Holy Spirit for each day's duties. A Christian without the anointing of the Holy Spirit is devoid of the essential of Christian living. A servant of the Lord

"Thou anointest my head with oil"

without the anointing is very soon detected: there is neither conviction nor power in his service, it is weak and sickly—in fact, he makes no progress in service because he is suffering from sunstroke. David said elsewhere that the sun should not strike us by day, nor the moon by night, because the Lord is our shade and our keeper. Sunstroke is weakness physically, and moonstroke is to be mentally and spiritually unbalanced. The anointing of the Holy Spirit will quicken the weak, and balance the unbalanced to spiritual sanctity.

We have climbed the mountains, now we come to the

**Valley.** This, too, can be an enemy. That is why David called it " The valley of the shadow of death ". Palestine is peculiarly a land of hills and valleys, some of the valleys being narrow and rugged defiles that abound with dangers. The enemy is not always seen, but the shadow tells of its possible presence. While we accompany our shepherd along this dangerous part of his journey, shall we think together of that fourth verse of the 23rd Psalm: " Yea, though I walk through the valley of the shadow of death, I will fear no evil: for Thou art with me." There are only two negatives in this Psalm, neither of which is detrimental to the Child of God. They are: " I shall not want," and " I will fear no evil ".

The verse opens with a doubt and that doubt concerns death. " Yea, though " not " when ". While one appreciates the fact that it has reference to the dangers of David's shepherd-life, yet we may draw from it an allusion or a spiritual significance that the second advent may have been the purport of the Holy Spirit, reminding us that some of us may not see death.

THE VALLEY OF SHADOW

Yet death is not the subject, it is in the valley of the SHADOW of death. A shadow would tell us that the monster itself is not far away for we cannot have shadow without substance, yet a shadow cannot hurt one. While this is true, yet these shadows ofttimes bring fear into the heart and many a soul has fainted at the sight of a shadow. Said David: "Though I be surrounded with these shadows, I will fear no evil: for Thou art with me." Try and imagine this valley to which David refers. He had brought his sheep down from a mountain-top into a deep ravine, a narrow path with rugged rocks on either side. As they journeyed there were caves out of which the robber might step, there were lairs from which the wild animal might spring. The lower they descended the darker it became, and the more formidable looked the towering cliffs and the overhanging rocks. Do you not see that the shadow of death was everywhere, and the monster might appear in one form or another, in a little slip or false step, in a falling rock or a springing animal? Certainly it was the kind of environment that would strike fear or terror into any heart. The sheep themselves did not see these things, all they saw and knew was the presence, and guidance, of their shepherd. So David looked up to the limited sky-line and reminded himself that he was as one of those sheep walking in dangerous places but, while he had a Shepherd, how could he fear harm!

How often we have walked through the valley of shadows, when death has lurked nearby. We see its shadow in the form of a motor-car, in sickness, in accidents we miss by inches—these things remind us of the uncertainty of life, in the midst of which we can walk calmly because we have His companionship.

The Psalmist said: "Yea, though I WALK." Here is a calm deliberate step such as would not suggest fear. He is not going to run through, neither is he going to stand still hesitantly to ponder over "maybe" or "perhaps". Even so, the Christian should have the confidence which would cause no alarm. "They shall not be confounded that trust in Thee."

Another important word in this verse is "through". David did not think of wandering IN the valley, but said: "Yea, though I walk THROUGH." This experience would only be a means to an end, just a temporal passing toward the glories of the beyond.

Our final thought here is the reason for our confidence. "THOU art with me." We are walking with One who knows every step of the way. He knows every danger, every temptation. He can make no mistake because He has said: "I am the Way." He will never lead me astray because He has said : "I am the Truth." He will never be overcome by death because He has said: "I am the Life." Death and its fears are swallowed up in victory.

Thus, with many and varied experiences, the shepherd leads his flock day after day: and so the Lord leads us through all the vicissitudes of life.

Because David experienced these dangers as a shepherd of the countryside, because he experienced evil threatenings at the hand of Saul in the palace, because his life was endangered from time to time as a King at the hand of both his enemies and his fellow-countrymen, he became the man who could definitely speak from

There were ninety and nine that safely lay
In the shelter of the fold,
But one was out on the hills away
Far off from the gates of gold ;
Away on the mountains wild and bare
Away from the tender Shepherd's care,
Away from the tender Shepherd's care.

" Lord, Thou hast here Thy ninety and nine,
Are they not enough for Thee ? "
But the Shepherd made answer : " This of Mine
Has wandered away from Me ;
And although the road be rough and steep
I go to the desert to find My sheep,
I go to the desert to find My sheep ".

But none of the ransomed ever knew
How deep were the waters crossed,
Nor how dark was the night that the Lord passed through
E'er He found His sheep that was lost,
Out in the desert He heard its cry,
Sick, and helpless, and ready to die,
Sick, and helpless, and ready to die.

" Lord, whence are those blood-drops all the way
That mark out the mountain track ? "
" They were shed for one who had gone astray
Ere the Shepherd could bring him back ".
" Lord, whence are Thy hands so rent and torn ?
They are pierced to-night by many a thorn,
They are pierced to-night by many a thorn ".

But all through the mountains, thunder-riven,
And up from the rocky steep,
There arose a cry to the gate of heaven :
" Rejoice ! I have found My sheep ".
And the angels echoed around the throne,
" Rejoice ! for the Lord brings back His own ! "
" Rejoice ! for the Lord brings back His own ! "

EASTERN SHEEPFOLD

experience. So it is that over and over again he repeats the injunction in the Psalms: "Fear not." "What time I am afraid, I will trust," " I will trust and not be afraid," or " I will not fear what man shall do unto me ". Let us confidently take the same stand amidst the calamitous days in which we live.

Not less precious are the lessons which we have yet to glean from our Bethlehem friends as we come to

## EVENTIDE

Darkness falls quite swiftly in the East, and protection must be made for the numerous flocks which are moving from place to place. Scattered over the land of Palestine are

### SHEEPFOLDS.

These are public property, just four low walls with an entrance at one corner and an enclosure in the opposite. The sheep, sometimes several flocks mixed up together, all sleep in the open part (as seen in the drawing), the enclosure is only for very severe weather, or lambing season when the sheep are with young. It is to be noticed that there is only an entrance and no door. That is because the folds are public. The shepherd, or if more than one flock, the shepherds, will take it in turns to become the door by filling up that entrance themselves, either standing in the doorway or lying across its threshold. Thus the statement in John 10 is literally and actually true: " I am the Door, by Me if any man enter in he shall be saved."

When the flock arrives at one of these folds in the eventide, the shepherd takes up his position in the doorway and, with his rod swinging up and down, he will allow it to fall lightly on the backs of the sheep as they pass inside in single file. It is what the Old Testament calls: " Passing under the rod." " And concerning the tithe of the herd, or of the flock, even of whatsoever passeth under the rod, the tenth shall be holy unto the Lord " (Lev. 27. 32).

As they pass in he is watching and should any one be limping, or look sickly, or show any signs of injury as blood stains, he draws such to his feet for attention. It sometimes happens that this checking up at the end of the day reveals that one of the lambs is missing. This will cause much concern to the shepherd who quickly ascertains which one it is, for he loves them all. If there are other shepherds he says to them: " Friends, I have lost one of my sheep." To this they express their sorrow. " Will you take my turn at being the door ? " " Yes," reply the sympathetic friends. If there should be no other shepherd at that fold, he engages an hireling or makes use of the " porter ". Then he equips himself for a return journey through the darkness to find that lost lamb. Here we are to see him use one other article of his equipment, namely his

THE RETURN OF THE LOST LAMB

## SHEPHERD'S LAMP

This has been described earlier in the book. Lighting up the little lamp inside, he sets forth holding the light to his feet. It was David who said elsewhere: "Thy Word is a lamp unto my feet, and a light unto my path." As he journeys he calls repeatedly and listens carefully. That lamb he is seeking may be a long way off from the track, or its bleat may be very faint owing to weakness. As he pursues his path he passes other sheepfolds. He had passed them earlier in the day but did not need their protection, but now they are occupied with other sheep and shepherds. So he calls to these shepherds: "Friends, have you seen my sheep which is lost?" "No," will possibly come back the answer, "But we hope you will find it." Thus he plods on perhaps only a little way, perhaps the best part of that day's journey. By and by he catches the first faint bleat, and with a light heart he alters his course and goes towards the cry. Finding the lamb he picks it up gently. Placing it upon his shoulders he again turns his feet towards the fold. Does he punish that lamb for bringing him out on such a journey when he was already tired? No! It has had its punishment, lost, lonely, cold, frightened, and hungry. On his journey back he again passes the folds and shepherds from whom he made enquiry. So now he calls to the same shepherds: "Rejoice with me; for I have found my sheep which was lost." Those shepherds will possibly sing and make merry for the rest of the night. But, you say, it was not one of their sheep. No! But it might have been, and they know that he loves his sheep as much as they love theirs.

Now with this scene in mind let us turn to the 15th chapter of Luke. There the Lord relates such an incident in parabolic form, applying it to the sinner. "And he spake this parable unto them, saying, What man of you, having an hundred sheep, if he lose one of them, doth not leave the ninety and nine in the wilderness, and go after that which is lost, until he find it? And when he hath found it, he layeth it on his shoulders, rejoicing. And when he cometh (is coming) home, he calleth together his friends and neighbours (the other shepherds), saying unto them, Rejoice with me; for I have found my sheep which was lost. I say unto you, that likewise joy shall be in heaven over one sinner that repenteth, more than over ninety and nine just persons, which need no repentance" (Luke 15. 3–7).

Having returned to the fold (possibly it is still dark), he takes the lamb from his shoulders and tucks it into his fleece coat, and together they lie down and sleep for the night. What a picture of the hymn we used to sing as children;—

> Jesus is our Shepherd, wiping every tear,
> Folded in His bosom, what have we to fear?"

When daylight arrives, he will look to see whether the lamb needs any attention. If not it is just put into the flock as though nothing had ever happened.

Are you a wandering sheep? Are you a backslider? If you are, will you see the grace and charm of this magnificent scene and know that Christ will treat you in just the same way? He will receive you, He will put you into the great flock of His saints, and you will be treated the same as the most faithful saint.

When David wrote this Psalm he was possibly sitting in some quiet retreat, resting his flock and gazing on them in meditation and reflection. Maybe while they laid about unconcerned he was thinking of the enemies he had encountered on their behalf, of the hardness they had endured, of the death he had faced, and now they had come through them into the place of victory and rest. There they were grazing without concern or fear: the wild animal may have been near, but they did not resist; the deep ravine may have brought death near to hand, but they had not seen it. Then, turning from these reflections, he set his eyes heavenwards and said: " The Lord is my Shepherd, I shall not want," or, as one version puts it: " Therefore can I lack nothing." What did these sheep lack if David were near? Nothing! What shall I lack if Jesus is near? Nothing! These sheep, thought David, lack nothing because I love them, I think for them, I do for them. Surely Jesus loves me, and interests Himself sufficiently in me to do for me. Shall not we who know Him thus join with David and say: " I shall not want ? "

I shall not want because Jesus has plenty. He is the source of supply. Every good and perfect gift cometh from above. He has promised to supply every need according to the riches of His glory in Christ Jesus. I shall not want because the Lord knows how to distribute His provisions. He will not give to one at the expense of another, nor meet one man's need and neglect the need of another. He is too wise to err, and is no respecter of persons. I must look to myself for the fault if there is one. Yet again—I shall not want protection because He is strong to defend and deliver. Whatever the form of the enemy, Christ is well able to meet it.

> He is able to deliver thee,
> He is able to deliver thee,
> Though by sin oppressed,
> Come to Him for rest,
> Our God is able to deliver thee.

It is sometimes good to look on the negative side of life because it helps us to appreciate the positive, especially if we are lacking in appreciation. Here are three pictures of want which we need to escape.

(1) *Belshazzar.* " Thou art weighed in the balances, and art found *wanting* " (Daniel 5. 27). He was a man who failed to live a god-like life. He rejected God and was later tried by God, and was found to be wanting before God. Such a man could not say: " The Lord is my Shepherd."

(2) *The Prodigal Son.* "And when he began to be in *want* " (Luke 15. 14). He had not always known the condition of want, and now that he did it was not his father's fault. He chose the selfish and independent life for himself; he wandered from the father's fold and the father's care. Distance meant want to him. The father's heart never changed; he still loved his son and longed for his return.

(3) *The Rich Man.* This man found himself in hell in *want* of salvation. He had never entered the fold from choice. He could have been saved, but would not. I trust that no reader of this booklet is in this dire need. If you are, learn that Jesus Christ, the Son of God, is a great and loving Shepherd, that He has gone out to meet you, and if you will receive His Love and appropriate His Salvation, He will receive you and give you salvation and assurance, enabling you to say: " The Lord is MY Shepherd, I shall not want," and then to sing:—

> All that I want is in Jesus,
> He satisfies, none else besides,
> Life would be worthless without Him,
> All things in Jesus I find.

## BENEDICTION

So the shepherd of Israel closes his Psalm with;
" Surely goodness and mercy shall follow me all the
days of my life; and I will dwell in the house of the
Lord for ever." What a wonderful bodyguard! What
a glorious retinue of servants! The Lord is going before
as Shepherd and Bodyguard, while these twin servants
follow up as a Rereward. Reminding ourselves of the
fact that we are only pilgrims, that we are being led,
and that our dwelling-place is yet to come, we will
consider this verse accordingly, seeing first :—

**The Pilgrim's Attendants.** Has it ever occurred
to you that you are ever surrounded and protected by
heavenly hosts ? Concerning angels, the Apostle says
in Hebrews 1. 14: " Are they not all ministering spirits,
sent forth to minister for them who shall be heirs of
salvation ? " Elisha prayed: " Lord, open his eyes,"
and his servant saw that they were surrounded with an
heavenly company. It has been beautifully expressed
that Goodness and Mercy are the names of two of
these heavenly attendants. Goodness follows us to
record all the good and noble things that we do,
registering them in heaven for reward; whilst Mercy
follows on, covering up all those things which are un-
Christlike, all our faults and failings, so that we " shall
not stand in the judgment ". It matters not where we
turn along life's way, there we see His goodness and
His mercy. Secondly, we have:

**The Pilgrim's Acknowledgment.** In his acknowledgment he shows an absolute certainty—"Surely," and declares an emphatic duration— "ALL the days of my life." It is not a case of some days goodness and some days evil, not mercy one day and judgment the next; but it is goodness and mercy every day and all the day, if so be we have learned, with the Apostle, how in every state of life therewith to be content. Some people can only see the goodness of the Lord on sunny days when things are bright and the path is smooth, just when things are as they would like them: but David had learned the same thing that was later expressed by the Apostle Paul that: "All things work together for good to them that love God." Thirdly, there is:—

**The Pilgrim's Anticipation.** "And I will dwell in the house of the Lord for ever." David, in the darkness of the old economy, seemed to have a glorious prospect of the future. We have to remember that David only had the first five books of the Bible—the Pentateuch—and in them there was no revelation of the future bliss. It is only in the New Testament that we are taught such truths as " In my Father's house are many mansions: if it were not so, I would have told you. I go to prepare a place for you. And if I go and prepare a place for you, I will come again, and receive you unto Myself; that where I am, there ye may be also." It is because we know we have a home yonder that we become conscious that here we have no abiding city, and so are only pilgrims and strangers. Finally, we have:—

**The Pilgrim's Assurance.** "And I WILL dwell in the house of the Lord for ever." No doubt with the Psalmist! He never said: " I may," or " I hope ", or " perhaps ", but " I WILL ". It is the assurance of faith. This is not one of the many experiences of life.

It is the ultimate consummation of the life that is hid with Christ in God. It is life indeed. The life present is the probationary period for the life that is to come.

" And I will dwell in the house of the Lord For Ever."

> For ever with the Lord,
> Amen, so let it be,
> Life from the dead is in that Word,
> 'Tis immortality.
> Here in the body pent,
> Absent from Him I roam,
> Yet nightly pitch my moving tent,
> A day's march nearer home.

# HE LEADETH ME

THE SHEPHERD'S ROD

# HE
# LEADETH
# ME

Shepherd Life in Palestine – Psalm 23

*By*

## C. W. SLEMMING

**CHRISTIAN LITERATURE CRUSADE**
Fort Washington, Pennsylvania 19034

CHRISTIAN LITERATURE CRUSADE

UNITED STATES
P. O. Box 1449, Ft. Washington, PA 19034


Copyright 1942 C.W. SLEMMING


First edition 1942
First North American edition 1965
Revised edition 1973


*ISBN 0-87508-505-9*

PRINTED IN THE UNITED STATES OF AMERICA

## PREFACE

TOO few people are acquainted with the habits and customs of Palestine, and so fail to obtain from the Scriptures the first lessons that they are meant to convey. It became my privilege, therefore, to write a little booklet on the Twenty-third Psalm entitled *Echoes from the Hills of Bethlehem*, which revealed much of the habit, custom, and equipment of the Eastern shepherd. This has gone into a number of issues and many testimonies of blessing have come from those who have read it.

With this encouragement the booklet has been enlarged so that the many references to the Shepherd throughout the Bible might be embraced. Many illustrations have now been included which make the book an attractive gift for Birthday, Anniversary, Christmas, for old or young, who will find comfort in the knowledge that the Good Shepherd is ever leading.

C. W. SLEMMING.

"Jesus said,
'I am the Good Shepherd'"

John 10. 11